CRESSIDA BELL'S
CAKE DESIGN

FIFTY FABULOUS CAKES

Photography: Sonja Read
Graphic Design: Alfonso Iacurci, Cultureshock Media
Production Manager: Nicola Vanstone, Cultureshock Media

Printed by Butler Tanner and Dennis Ltd, U.K.

Double-Barrelled Books
28A Finborough Road,
London SW10 9EG
T: + 44 (0) 7768 583 824

Distributed by:
Thames & Hudson
181A High Holborn, London WC1V 7QX
T: +0) 207 7845 5000
F: +44 (0) 20 7845 5050

A CIP catalogue record for this book is available from the British Library
ISBN 978-0-9571500-3-4

CRESSIDA BELL'S
CAKE DESIGN

FIFTY FABULOUS CAKES

Photographs by Sonja Read

DOUBLE-BARRELLED
BOOKS

CONTENTS

FOREWORD

There are so many reasons to welcome Cressida Bell's extraordinary and inspiring decorations for cakes, but the first is relief. At last, I thought. The adornment of celebration cakes has been mired in a menu of sugar flowers and cute animals for too long, the art being long overdue for a gale of fresh air. And here it is, in an energetic stream of edible mosaics and clashes of colour; a joyful mix of wit and seriousness. My next and perhaps happiest response to her designs was that they are do-able. As I am someone who has never had the steady hand to pipe a shell of royal icing, let alone write "Happy Birthday" neatly onto a cake, Cressida's appliquéd sugar formations suit the abilities of my own hands. I could contentedly sit cutting, moulding and arranging these patterns with all the pleasure of a child given its first pair of scissors and a stack of coloured paper, and I believe many others, of every age, will be inspired to try too. This book takes us into a new era of cake fashion, but one that should not intimidate, only bring endless delight.

Rose Prince

INTRODUCTION

In our house when we were children, Christmas had quite a touch of Victoriana. We had real candles on the tree and were only allowed to see this lit-up spectacle after tea on Christmas Day. The cake with this tea was always decorated by my father, Quentin, and it was always very splendid. He used quantities of silver and gold balls, glacé cherries, angelica, crystallised violets and rose petals, and the results were quite unlike any of the other festive offerings I had seen. Unlike many children growing up I didn't have much of a sweet tooth, so my main interest in his cakes was aesthetic. I do remember enjoying the occasional stolen cherry – and even some marzipan – but fruit cake was not my thing. Quentin was a great decorator – he painted our walls with patterned sponge prints, designed beautiful birthday cards and made us individual pottery cups with our names on. When I was eight we moved near to Duncan Grant's house, Charleston, in Sussex and on our regular visits no doubt I absorbed some of the joie de vivre of the house style. I suppose it is unsurprising then that my enthusiasm for all things decorative emerged at quite a young age.

Until my early teenage years I had dreams of being a jeweller but then I turned my ambitions towards textile design, which I still do, amongst other things. All forms of decoration and adornment fascinate me so it was natural that at some point I should turn my attention towards cakes. Over the years I have become the principal cake decorator in my family, taking over the role from Quentin when he became too old, and as my nephews and nieces grew up and became less keen to help I was able to graduate from the earlier more child-friendly cakes and make the designs increasingly elaborate. The ritual of decorating the cake on Christmas Eve while listening to Carols from Kings on the radio is now enshrined in tradition in our house – though the cake now takes much more time than the service.

Design for a Lutyens-inspired wall-hanging

I often look for new Ingredients and ideas on my travels; Warhol-style flowers, Turkish carnations, Arizona cacti, a madonna and child and Sicilian marzipan fruits have all featured in my designs. I will turn my hand to cakes on many different themes – but I don't really go in for cakes that look like something else – a doll or a snail or whatever. I want a cake to look like a cake, wonderfully over-the-top but still recognisably a cake.

I prefer to use only edible Ingredients – it seems such a shame to remove the ornaments before serving – and although I rarely actually eat any cake myself, ideally I also want the decorations to be delicious. The best tasting cakes to me are those covered with marzipan and glacé fruit but icing these days comes in such wonderful colours it is hard to resist using it in quantities. Luckily a lot of people do actually like eating it!

The revival of old fashioned sweets has been another great source of inspiration – and there are so many wonderful sugar baubles, beads and sprinkles available on the internet that it is hard to know where to start. I have ended up with quite a collection – silver balls in all different sizes, bags of pastel sweets, glacé cherries in green, yellow and three shades of red and all sorts of exotic crystallised fruit. There is now a whole drawer full of colourful sparkling decorations in my studio and I wake in the night thinking of new ways to use them!

The cakes in this book are intended more to inspire than instruct. I have tried to explain how each design was conceived and created but I did not want to write a very exacting step by step guide. I don't, after all, expect everyone to have the time and patience to spend hours sorting sugar balls into different sizes in the way that I do. I do hope though, that with this book I have managed to convey my joy and pleasure in the creation of each cake decoration and that they will inspire you as well as amaze and delight.

Cressida Bell

BEFORE YOU START

If you are thinking of creating one of the designs shown in this book it is essential that you read this first! The instructions are not repeated for each individual cake.

By profession I am a designer rather than a cake decorator and I think it would be fair to say that I have very little ability with piping or icing, so I started from a no-skills basis. I think that if I can do it, then, with patience and a following wind, anybody can. If you have ever drawn or painted then you can certainly create the sort of decoration that I show in this book. Think of it as applied art; the application of a pattern or a design onto a flat surface.

I look on the cake as a blank canvas. I start by seeing the cake in front of me as simply a circle or a square and then I think about what sort of pattern or design will work within that shape. All the decorations that I use are edible and readily available – it's just a matter of combining the different elements and sticking them on to the cake.

I have gradually collected what I consider to be my essential equipment for creating a design and applying it to the cake. Although you can use my list as a guide, over time you will probably discover what you find necessary in your own set of tools. Most items are readily available in the home but you may need to buy a few more.

The silver balls indicate the degree of difficulty, with five indicating the most difficult.

The fondant cream indicates where and how children can join in.

EQUIPMENT

Turntable
This not absolutely necessary but very useful. My father used his potter's wheel but turntables in different sizes are available quite cheaply from specialist suppliers.

Paper
You will need some heavy weight cartridge paper or card for making templates. It can also be made into a useful tool when cut in the shape of a circle and used to slide beneath the icing shapes so as to place them accurately onto the cake. You may also need layout paper or other lightweight paper on which you can draw your design. You can then prick through it easily to transfer the pattern directly onto the cake. Remember your piece of paper will need to be as large as your cake.

Ruler and large set square
Any type will do but I prefer to use a metric grader's square because it is a brilliant design tool with many uses.

Pencils, needles and pins
A selection of these will be useful for drawing, marking out your design and attaching it to the cake.

Scissors
You will need them to cut paper and gold leaf.

Chopping boards
You should have at least two, one for rolling out and the other for cutting and slicing.

Rolling pin
A large one is necessary not only for rolling out but for moving and lifting the icing and marzipan.

Kitchen knives
These are needed for cutting and moving icing, marzipan, glacé fruits and anything else of your choice.

Palette knife
A large one is particularly good for smoothing the icing and for moving more cumbersome pieces.

Artist's scalpel
This should be one with a small, sharp point for cutting out fiddly shapes in icing. A snap-off craft knife would work but is not as good.

Small containers
Use an assortment of saucers and pots to decant your smaller decorations into.

Tweezers
The flat-headed variety are the most useful for picking up and placing small decorations.

Paint brushes

I use paint brushes rather than pastry brushes for applying edible glue, wetting surfaces and painting on colours.

Tape measure

This may be necessary for measuring around the cake.

A jug of hot water, kitchen roll and dish cloths

These are to clean up with while you work and afterwards.

A cake board or platter

You will need something to display the cake on once it is finished!

INGREDIENTS AND HOW TO USE THEM

I prefer to use only edible ingredients. More and more of the ingredients that I use to decorate my cakes can be found in supermarkets but specialist suppliers and online companies now provide fantastic decorations in a range of colours and styles unavailable elsewhere. See the list of suppliers on p152.

Glaze

It is usual for cakes to be covered with an apricot glaze before icing to prevent crumbs creeping into the decoration.

Marzipan

Marzipan is not essential but for most cakes it is another useful anti-crumb barrier between the cake and the icing. It also provides a smooth surface on which to spread your icing. I regularly make my designs almost entirely out of marzipan because my family do not like icing at all. An example of this is Bloomsbury Bouquet (p.72). The background is of plain white marzipan, with colouring added to make the stems and vase.

Home-made marzipan tastes best, but the bought variety (in white or yellow) can be useful for detailed work as it is smoother and takes colour better.

Icing

It is generally easiest to used ready-made fondant icing as it remains soft and malleable longer than the home-made variety. It is widely available in supermarkets and comes in block form or ready-rolled. They also sell quite a wide range of colours, including black. Some taste better than others so you may want to try them first!

You can adjust the colour of the icing with food colouring; there are specialist concentrated icing colourings, which may be easier to use, but ordinary food colouring will do. Remember though that the more food colouring you use, the wetter the icing will become, so you will need to add more icing sugar or leave it to dry out for a while. You can also mix coloured icings together to achieve a greater variety and subtlety of shades. They have to be kneaded well to ensure an even tone.

Frosting

I was brought up to use the term buttercream, but due to the recent upsurge in the popularity of cupcakes this is now generally known as frosting, so I will use that term in this book. If I want a thick, fluffy base for the cake decoration I use frosting, either making my own or buying the ready-made variety. Icing or no icing, marzipan or no marzipan – the choice is yours. The fruit cakes on page 120 and 126 have no icing of any sort, and the fruit topped ones on pages 92 and 106 have frosting as a base. It is largely a matter of taste, and also depends on the type of design.

Writing icing

I find ready-to-use writing icing much more convenient than the traditional piping bag. It comes in a range of ready-made colours but experts may find it relatively crude in comparison with piped icing. Writing icing is also useful to draw outlines for designs (Peacock Cake p.112) or to make spots (Gold Star cake p.90).

Cornflour

This is more useful than icing sugar when rolling out the icing.

Food colouring

This can be bought either in traditional liquid form, as a gel or as a paste. The choice and variety of colours is wide.

Glacé fruit

I love to use glacé fruit. Firstly, they taste good and are 'real'. Secondly, they are both colourful and lustrous. Thirdly, they add an extra dimension if they are used whole. They can be horrendously sticky to chop up, but if you keep a bowl of hot water handy this can be easily alleviated.

Red glacé cherries are an obvious choice; in green and yellow they are a bit more unusual (see list of suppliers p.152). Candied peel can be used to great effect (Goldfish cake p.60 and Dahlia Cake p.106) and angelica is invaluable when bought in its natural long-stemmed state. It can be used for flower stalks and to outline geometric shapes (Klimt Cake p.132). Crystallised whole red pears, mandarins, figs, pineapples and kiwi slices can be spectacular when simply stuck on a fruit cake (Fruit & Nut cake p.126 and Mellow Fruit cake p.120) or when used literally in a design such as Frutero (p.122).

Dragees and silver balls

The term 'dragee' is used to mean many things, but in this book it refers to the large almond shaped coloured or gilded sweets which contain either chocolate or almonds (also known as sugared almonds). Silver and gold balls come in various sizes. You can also find coloured sugar balls, non-pareils and mimosa balls as well as sugar covered hearts in pink, gold and red. Other possibilities may include polka dots, sugar pearls and sugar glitter. The choice is enormous.

Sweets

I have found several suppliers who specialise in many varieties of old-fashioned sweets (see list of suppliers p.152) and once you start looking at what is available all sorts of design ideas present themselves. Sweets like mini-Easter eggs, pastel-coloured fondants, jelly beans, Liquorice Allsorts, Smarties and gobstoppers all provide me with new inspiration for cake designs.

Edible glue

This is a ready-to-use liquid glue derived from natural plant gums which is indispensable when attaching decoration to the cakes and is widely available online.

Jewels

Using a sugar substitute called isomalt, which does not caramelize, you can make your own sugar gemstones fairly easily by melting the isomalt, adding colour and pouring into special moulds. Full instructions can be found online when you buy the supplies (see list of suppliers p.152). You can also buy ready-made jewels of either isomalt or jelly (see list of suppliers p.152). Either way, jewels are best applied at the last minute or they will cloud over. The jelly variety is longer lasting.

You can also substitute sweets for jewels. Try midget gems or hard-boiled shiny sweets like glacier fruits and mints that you can break up.

Nuts

Pecans, almonds and hazelnuts taste good, look good and can be gilded for extra effect.

Gold leaf

Edible gold leaf can be used to great effect for an extra grand cake. It is best cut with a pair of sharp scissors and stuck with edible glue. Beware though, it is incredibly light and floats away at the slightest breath.

Gold paint

Where gold leaf is impractical or too expensive try using gold paint. They vary in quality and you may need two coats to get anything resembling gold. I have tried the gold pens too, but so far haven't found a satisfactory one.

Further suggestions:

Printed icing

There are many websites that offer to print your imagery onto icing for you. Generally these seem to be used to make photo cakes. You can however search for lovely patterns on the internet and have them printed out instead. These could even become a base for yet more decoration. A simple printed design could be adorned with cherries, fruit and gold balls with no need for you to draw anything.

Flowers

Crystallised or sugared wild and garden flowers like violas, nasturtiums and lavender are available from specialist suppliers, and can be used en masse.

THE DESIGN

Start working on your design before you prepare the cake for decoration. The design for a new cake can come from either an idea already in your head or a visual reference or interesting ingredients that you have found.

Drawing

Depending on the type and difficulty of the design, I usually draw my idea out in sketch form first, so that I can see what I'm doing. If it is a complex design, I then draw it out full size on a piece of paper that I have cut to the same size as the cake. I can then transfer the design by attaching the paper to the cake with a few pins, then pricking the design through onto the icing or marzipan.

Templates

I often use templates cut out of card or paper, as in, for instance, the Baubles Cake (p.134) or the leaves on Thanksgiving Cake (p.124). Any shape that you will want to repeat is much more easily done this way. Once you have cut out the shape in paper, position it on your rolled-out icing and cut around it with a scalpel.

Computer images

A computer can also come in useful here. If you have a photo or design programme, you can find lots of ready-made shapes which you can print, cut out and use for templates. You could even print out a particular image from the internet and use that instead of designing your own.

Writing

For any writing I find my computer essential. Rather than drawing out my own letters I look for a font I like and print out the words to the right size. Then I cut the letters out and use them as a template (Happy Birthday p.44 & Noel Cake p.136)). Generally a font without serifs is best – don't make it too hard for yourself!

Basic designs

One of the easiest of designs to make is probably a pattern of concentric circles, for which you could use a single simple ingredient; glacé cherries in different colours for example, or different types of sweet like on the Flying Saucers cake (p.42). Start from the centre and arrange the decorations in ever increasing circles. A radiating star is also a relatively easy motif, of which there are several examples in the book. Another easy design could be a simple geometric pattern, which you would need to measure out first onto the cake, working out where everything should go before you start.

Inspiration

Inspiration can come from everywhere. I often find myself looking at something and wondering how it could be transformed into a pattern fitting into a circle or a square. Might a snowflake work, or a constellation ? The sun and moon? I thought up the Kremlin Crown cake, for example, (p.84) because I was in the Museum in Moscow and saw the Tsars' crowns which looked just like cakes.

A design often starts with the ingredients that you have found, maybe in sweet shops, markets or bazaars. Part of the fun is looking out for things you might use as decorations; sugared almonds, chocolate buttons, marzipan fruit?

You should take my designs as a starting point but go further. Try a cake covered with nothing but serried ranks of pink sugar mice perhaps, or dolly mixtures arranged into a chequerboard. Personally, I tend to go for things that shine and sparkle a bit like the Catherine Wheel (p.36). In fact, since finishing the photography for this book, I've thought it would be fun to do a Snakes and Ladders cake, making icing squares and using jelly snakes and liquorice ladders. You will find that once you start thinking this way you will have no end of ideas. Be bold, it's only a cake!

When you have decided on your decorative ingredients, line them up, see what you've got and think how you're going to use them. The chocolate cake (Chocolate Box p.96) is a good example of this. I bought lots of packets of different chocolates; buttons in three colours, Matchmakers, chocolate oranges and stars, then worked out how they could be arranged to best effect.

Children
Some of the designs in this book are more child-friendly than others and I have marked these up as such on the relevant pages. The idea is to involve the children and try not to be too controlling. The end result does not have to look perfect – it's the participation that counts here.

CONSTRUCTION

Once you have your design worked out on paper, or at least in your head, and you are surrounded by your decorative elements, it is time to assemble everything.

PREPARATION
Think of a cake like a blank canvas, which needs preparation before you can start work. You generally need a smooth base on which to create your design; this can be glazed, marzipan, icing or frosting, or a combination of these. At the very least you should use a glaze to provide a barrier against cake crumbs.

After glazing, if you are using marzipan it should be rolled out to a size big enough to cover the cake entirely and draped over it, easing the sides down without creasing. Some cakes are smoother than others; fruit cakes, for example, can be fairly rugged, so when using marzipan it needs to be pressed into the crevices by hand and then smoothed out with the help of a rolling pin.

Icing the cake is done in a similar fashion. Roll it out and drape it over, trimming off the excess neatly around the base.

DECORATION

Icing

If you are using icing for the decoration, choose the colours you need and roll out enough for the shape you want, using cornflour on both the board and the rolling pin to stop the icing sticking. It should be rolled fairly thin but not so much so as to make it fragile.

The trick here is to roll out the icing and let it dry a bit before you cut your shapes so that it is not as stretchy and soft as it was when first rolled. It is then quite easy to cut your shapes using a template or ruler. When you have cut your shapes out they will still be quite soft and pliable. Leave them a little longer so that they firm up and become easier to manoeuvre into place. If you need to leave them for hours on end, cover them with paper or film to keep them from becoming brittle.

Icing can be rolled into very slim 'bootlaces' (See Starburst p.32) with the help of a large set square or other sheet of rigid plastic. This should preferably be see-through so you can see what you are doing. Start rolling by hand on a cornfloury board. Once you have made a slim sausage shape swap to using the set square, keeping it parallel to the board. As the roll lengthens you can cut or break it in half to keep it manageable. Keep rolling and dividing until you have the size and quantity of rolls you need. If the icing is quite dry it can become too brittle; trial and error will help you find the right consistency. Marzipan can also be treated in the same way (see Bloomsbury Bouquet p.72).

To stick the icing shapes into place, just wet the icing or marzipan base with a paint brush and put them into place – they'll stick. Do likewise with things like glacé cherries and other sticky fruit – they usually just stay put.

Baubles

For silver balls, jewels, sweets and much else, a pot of edible glue is wonderful. You just paint the glue along the outline of your design and then place your ingredients on to the glue. When the glue dries it is transparent, so you don't even have to be that neat. The Kimono Cake (p.54) is an example of a design secured with edible glue.

Sides

If you want to decorate the sides of the cake you will need to use glue and even pins to keep things in place until the glue dries. Alternatively, you can leave the sides free of decoration, which is what I often do. If I do have to extend the design down the sides, I try to keep them as simple as possible. Sometimes I make a ribbon of coloured icing, measuring the cake and then rolling out a long strip and cutting it to size. I then roll it up and glue it on to the edge, unrolling as I go along. Otherwise a line of glacé cherries or other striking decorations will do the trick.

Fruit

The fruit decoration cakes are fun to do and relatively easy. There is no real need for icing or marzipan. If it is one of the fresh fruit versions apply an apricot glaze first and then a layer of frosting or whipped cream as a base for the fruit. If it is a fruit cake decorated with glacé fruit and nuts a simple glaze will suffice. Either set up the fruit design onto a board and then transfer it into place or arrange the pieces of fruit directly onto the cake.

Nuts

You can gild pecans or almonds with gold leaf to add glamour to your decoration. First paint the nuts with edible glue, then lay them onto a sheet of gold leaf. They can then be cut apart with scissors and trimmed of any excess. Finally use a dry paintbrush to burnish the surface.

Finishing

When you have finished your cake you may want to clean off any excess cornflour by painting the icing with a little clean water. This will take around 12 hours to dry completely but will restore the colour and brighten the cake.

Disasters

Although I have had trouble with hand-written icing and piping it is actually quite difficult to have a disaster, as everything you are doing is so basic and can simply be removed and begun again. Glue is also good for removing mistakes. If a colour has run or you have a mess of some sort, try painting on some glue. If you then wash and dry your brush and use it to wipe off the glue, surprisingly the stray colour will come with it. You can also chase up stray silver balls and sprinkles using a gluey brush.

Icing can crack if dried out too quickly so after you have finished do not put it in front of the fire to dry the final glue and water. Once decorated, the cakes last well, particularly if the base is a fruit one, so there is no need to rush them to table. You have blanketed them with icing so they are pretty well preserved.

Above all, be pragmatic! If you find that you are running out of something, rethink what you are doing and add something else. It's always worth buying more of everything than you think you will need. Decorations last almost indefinitely so they will not go to waste.

Decorating a cake in this way is rather like embroidery; you do need patience and some dexterity but it is also a very satisfying way to spend some time. It takes me a few hours to decorate a cake: there are no short cuts. You don't have to make the designs as elaborate as I have done though. I am both a perfectionist and a bit of an over-decorator but you can easily think of ways of simplifying things to suit your own purposes.

RECIPES

Baking is not really my field so Rose Prince has kindly supplied these five delicious recipes. If you want your cake to taste as good as it looks this is the best place to start.

Chocolate Sponge
Makes 2 × 20cm cakes, to sandwich with buttercream before decoration.

To make 2 × 30cm cakes double all quantities except baking powder (use 3tsp).

- 450g unsalted butter, softened
- 450g caster sugar
- 8 medium eggs
- 350g self-raising flour, sifted
- 100g cocoa powder, sifted
- 3 tsp baking powder, sifted
- 1/2 tsp fine sea salt
- 2 tsp vanilla extract
- 200ml whole milk

Preheat the oven to 170°C/Gas 4 and butter the tins. Place the butter and sugar in a stand mixer and beat until pale coloured and increased in volume. Add all the remaining ingredients at once, sifting in the flour with the baking powder. Beat the cake mixture for about 3 minutes until it turns lighter in colour and appears more voluminous.

Divide the mixture between 2 cake tins and smooth the surface with a knife and bake for 35-45 minutes until a skewer inserted in the centre comes out clean. It is important to check that this cake is properly cooked or it will fall after baking. Even if the skewer comes out clean, it is a good idea to 'listen' to the cake. If you can hear a sizzling sound, it needs further cooking; if not, it is cooked through. This mixture is also ideal for making individual chocolate cakes in paper cases.

Rich Fruit Cake

Makes a fruity, juicy cake that must be cooked very slowly so that the outer surface remains soft. Insulate the tin well with layers of paper.

Equipment: 30cm cake tin with loose base (see cake tin preparation, below). You can also use a 23cm cake tin which will result in a thicker cake.

- 250g unsalted butter
- 250g soft light brown sugar
- 200g plain flour, sifted
- 50g ground almonds
- 4 eggs
- 1 tsp ground allspice
- 1 tsp ground mixed spice
- 1 dessert apple, grated
- 1 tbsp molasses
- zest of 1 orange
- 50g whole almonds
- 100g currants
- 100g sultanas
- 100g dried figs, sliced
- 150g large raisins
- 100g pitted prunes, chopped
- 100g dried apricots, chopped
- Brandy or whisky to 'feed' the cake (optional)

To glaze the cake before decoration: 4 tbsp marmalade, simmered with 2 tbsp water, then passed through a sieve to make a clear glaze.

Butter inside of cake tin, then line base with a circle of baking parchment. Cut a long piece of baking paper (enough to go around the tin once) about 15cm in width. Fold in half and secure it inside the tin to form a cylinder of paper. It should adhere to the buttered sides of the tin. Butter the inside again, then dust with plain flour. Cut a second piece that goes twice around the tin and wrap this around the outside, to the same height as the inner strip, this time securing by tying it with a piece of string. Preheat the oven to 140°C/Gas 1.

Put the butter and sugar in a large mixing bowl – an electric mixer will help – and beat until the mixture increases in volume and is pale in colour. Have ready the flour and ground almonds. With the beater running, add 4 eggs, one at a time, adding a dessertspoonful of the flour and ground almonds after each egg has been added. Fold in the rest of the flour and almonds with the allspice and mixed spice.

Stir in apple and molasses, add the orange zest. Finally add the almonds and stir in all the dried fruit. Spoon the mixture into the tin.

Bake the cake for about 4-5 hours. Test to see if the cake is done by inserting a skewer. If it comes out clean, it is ready. Cool in the tin for about 45 minutes, then remove and allow to cool completely before wrapping in greaseproof paper and then clingfilm.

You can 'feed' the cake with brandy or whisky: drizzle 2 tbsp over the surface once a week and re-wrap with paper and clingfilm. This cake will keep for up to 2 months in a sealed container.

Plain Cake Sponge

Makes one 25cm cake; 5cm depth or one 30cm cake; 4cm depth.

Ideal for decoration, this sponge has a firm texture that can bear the weight of fondant icing, yet a velvety texture and lovely flavour of butter.

Stores for 5 days refrigerated/2 days room temperature/2 months frozen.

- 150g clarified butter *noisette* – see below
- 8g vanilla essence
- 446g egg yolks (about 10-12 egg yolks)
- 350g caster sugar
- 200g sifted plain flour
- 58g cornflour
- 120g cold water

Preheat the oven to 180°C/Gas 4. To make the clarified butter bring 250g unsalted butter to the boil and allow to simmer gently until the butter smells fragrantly nutty and the solids at the bottom of the pan are pale brown. Remove from the heat immediately and pass through a fine sieve. Discard the solids and add the vanilla to the clear, light brown clarified butter; set aside, keeping the butter warm so that it remains liquid.

Put yolks and sugar into a large mixing bowl placed over a pan of barely boiling water and use a hand held electric whisk to mix until the mixture is pale and foamy and nearly triple the original volume.

Mix the flour with the cornflour and set aside. Decrease speed of mixing and add the cold water.

Add half of the blended flours to the egg mixture then use a large balloon whisk to fold quickly and lightly into the flour. When the flour disappears, repeat with the rest of the flour mixture.

Pour the clarified butter into the mixture then fold in with the whisk – as before. Make sure that this is done thoroughly before pouring the cake batter into the prepared tin. Bake for 45-60 minutes until the cake is golden brown on the surface and feels springy to the touch. As soon as the cake is cooked, turn out on to a rack.

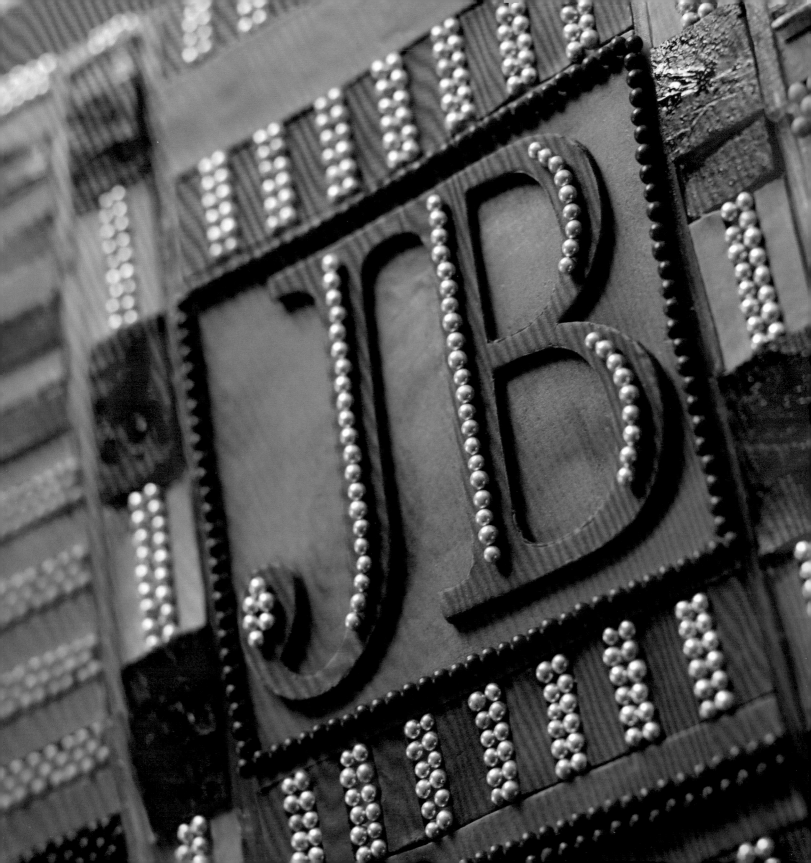

Buttercream

*For a single layer of buttercream on a
30cm cake:*

- 100g unsalted butter, softened
- 100g icing sugar, sifted
- 1 egg yolk

Put the butter and icing sugar in a large
mixing bowl and beat until the volume
increases and the mixture is paler in colour.
Add the egg yolk and beat for a further 2
minutes for a lighter and airier buttercream.
Spread onto the cake with a palette knife.
The buttercream can be stored in the fridge
for up to 3 days, but allow to soften at room
temperature before using.

Added flavourings
- Vanilla – add 1 tsp of vanilla extract
- Chocolate – add 30g cocoa powder
- Orange – add the zest of 1 orange
- Coffee – combine 1 tsp instant coffee with
  1 tsp boiling hot water
- Rose – add 1 tsp natural rose flavouring
- Praline – add 50g finely ground toasted
  hazelnuts, or hazelnut paste
- Pistachio – add 50g finely ground unsalted
  pistachio nuts

Marzipan

*This recipe will make 1kg marzipan.
Make it the day before use as it will be
easier to roll.*

- 180g caster sugar
- 280g icing sugar
- 450g ground almonds
- 2 medium eggs
- 1 egg yolk

Put the sugar, icing sugar and almonds in
a bowl and mix together. Add the eggs and
egg yolk, mix lightly then turn out onto the
worktop. Push the mixture together with your
hands until it forms a dough, then knead until
it is malleable and smooth. You may need
to dust the worktop with a little more icing
sugar if the dough sticks to it. Wrap tightly in
clingfilm, then store.

Marzipan flavours
- 1 tsp vanilla extract or the
  seeds scraped from 1 vanilla pod
- The zest of either 1 orange or lemon
- 1 tsp rosewater or orange
  flower water
- 2 tsp almond liqueur

CHRISTENINGS

STARBURST

23cm diameter

This cake is based on a textile design of mine called 'Celestial' which has hundreds of small stars like this in an all-over repeat.

Ingredients

- Marzipan
- Black icing
- White icing
- Yellow icing in two shades
- Yellow sugar pearls
- Blue sugar pearls
- Edible glue

This design makes use of two star templates for the double layered star in two shades of yellow. The radiating lines are made of thinly rolled black icing and continue down the sides of the cake. The shimmering blue pearls are gradually spaced out to add to the starburst effect.

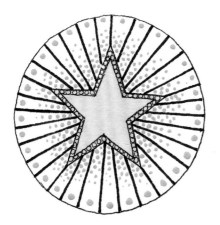

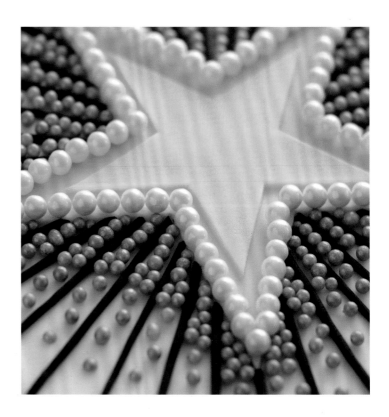

CONSTELLATION CAKE

30cm diameter

Ingredients
- Marzipan
- Pink icing
- Blue icing
- White icing
- Mauve dragees
- White sugar pearls
- Edible glue

The white icing ovals have to fit into the blue circles like a jigsaw. Probably the easiest way to do this is to work out the whole pattern first on paper. If you then cut out the blue and white shapes based on the drawing they should fit together easily. I tried to do it as I went along which made things very difficult. The easy bit is to stick on the dragees and pearls at the end.

I have used this design on many things from scarves to furniture but I think using it as a cake decoration was pushing it to the limit. For a simple pattern it was very hard to execute!

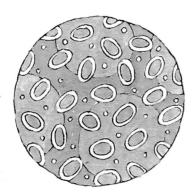

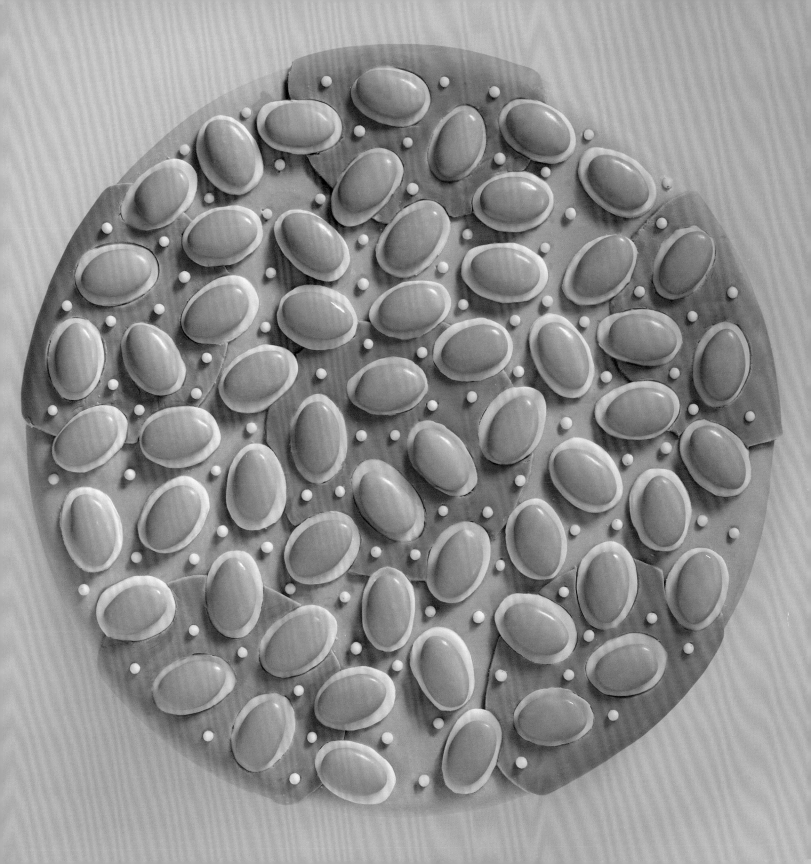

CATHERINE WHEEL

30cm diameter

Ingredients

- Marzipan
- White icing
- Silver edible paint
- Gold dragees
- Silver dragees
- Blue dragees
- Pink chocolate hearts
- Silver sugar balls
- Sugar pearls
- Edible glue

This is just a curvy version of a starburst design. If you mark out the middle and ends of a star you can then use a curved template (draw around a plate) to join the dots. Once you have drawn these lines you paint the whole thing silver and press in the decorations.

Children can press the dragees in once you have drawn the lines

I originally did this cake in red, gold and silver on an un-iced fruit cake. In the middle were star shaped sparklers which we lit on Christmas day.

ANGEL WINGS

30cm diameter

Ingredients

- Marzipan
- Pale blue icing
- Pale pink icing
- White icing
- Pale pink sugar balls
- Pale green sugar balls
- Large, medium and tiny silver sugar balls
- Clear isomalt jewels
- Edible glue

I drew out two templates for the wings here; one goes on top of the other. The other white icing flourishes were cut freehand, but you could make a template for these as well. I sorted my silver balls into size (they vary quite a bit in each pack) so I could embellish the wings with graded silver beads. The finishing touches were in adding the pink and green balls and the clear jewels.

For inspiration when trying to think of a christening cake I looked at a bible cover designed by Duncan Grant. It was painted with angels wings which seemed just the thing – for either a girl or a boy.

CHILDREN'S BIRTHDAYS

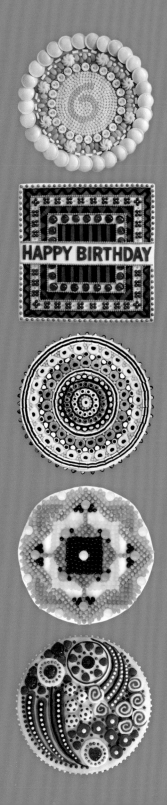

FLYING SAUCERS

30cm diameter

Ingredients

- Marzipan
- Blue-green icing
- Flying saucers
- Refreshers
- Fondant creams
- Jelly beans
- White candy sticks
- White mimosa balls
- Pink sugar balls
- Orange sugar balls
- Turquoise sugar balls
- Yellow and green sugar polka dots
- Edible glue

You need to get quite a few bags of flying saucers if you want to limit yourself to only two colours as I have done here. Once you have picked out your number in polka dots (you will have to trim some to fit) you can just work outwards adding the sweets of your choice. Surprisingly the flying saucers stuck down (and together) quite well. I added a few more coloured balls to brighten the colour scheme a bit.

Children might help to add (and eat) the refreshers, fondant creams and jelly beans

I always liked these sherbet flying saucers best out of all the penny sweets available when I was little. I thought they would taste great with refreshers (more sherbet) and then added a load of other pastel coloured sweets to make a great child-friendly cake.

HAPPY BIRTHDAY

30cm square

Ingredients

- Marzipan
- Pink icing
- White icing
- Black icing
- Red icing
- Black writing icing
- Black sugar pearls
- Red sugar balls
- Turquoise sugar balls
- Gold balls
- Pink pearls
- Red glacé cherries
- Edible glue

There is a bit of geometry necessary here in order to fit the pink and white icing strips together neatly. If you draw it all out and use templates this should not be too difficult. Also, once the decorations are put on top no-one will know if there were gaps! In order to fit the triangles , wiggles and squares into the spaces for them you will have to either work it all out first or use trial and error. The writing is done on a computer as always, the letters being printed and cut out and then used as a template for the red icing.

I made a silk bandana some years ago with a design similar to this. It consists of some simple patterns in a series of borders with Happy Birthday emblazoned across the middle.

ALLSORTS CAKE

30cm diameter

Ingredients

- Marzipan
- White icing
- Liquorice Allsorts
- Liquorice fruit sticks in yellow, pink and green
- Liquorice creams
- Liquorice mints
- Liquorice wheels
- Bubble gum millions
- Liquorice coconut rolls
- Edible glue

To eke out the Ingredients most of the sweets are cut in half or into slices. The black circular lines are made of unrolled liquorice wheels and the turquoise spots are bubble gum millions. It is a fairly straightforward design but you do have to trim the rectangular Allsorts slightly to make a circle. I started at the edge with the black and white mints and then worked inwards, spacing my Ingredients by trial and error before sticking them down.

Children should be able to do most of this if they have a little help cutting up the Allsorts.

Liquorice Allsorts are the most strikingly graphic looking sweets. Ever since I got hold of some Bassetts special promotional fabric when I was a teenager I have loved the way they look. They seem to me an obvious choice for decorating a cake.

JELLY BEAN CAKE

30cm diameter

Ingredients
- Marzipan
- White icing
- Jelly beans (about 800gms)
- Gobstoppers
- Edible glue

It is surprising how many jelly beans you need to cover the top of a cake if they are placed end up. I had expected to have enough but finished with some gaps. Don't buy them in equal quantities; you need more of the outer colours. If in doubt buy extra – I'm sure they will get eaten somehow. The design is quite a simple geometric one which you can rule out straight onto the cake. Use thick icing and marzipan so that there is enough depth to stick the jelly beans into, then just stick them in according to the pattern.

This should be fun for children to help with once you have marked out the triangles.

Seeing a huge display of colourful jelly beans in a department store inspired me to do this cake. The colours were so fabulous and I spent ages picking out the most vibrant ones.

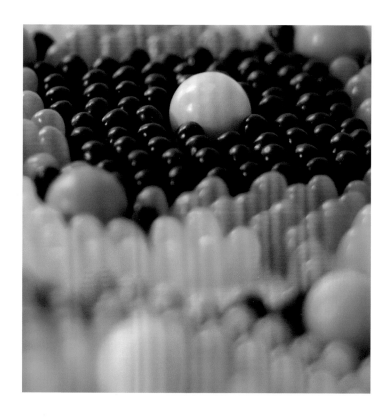

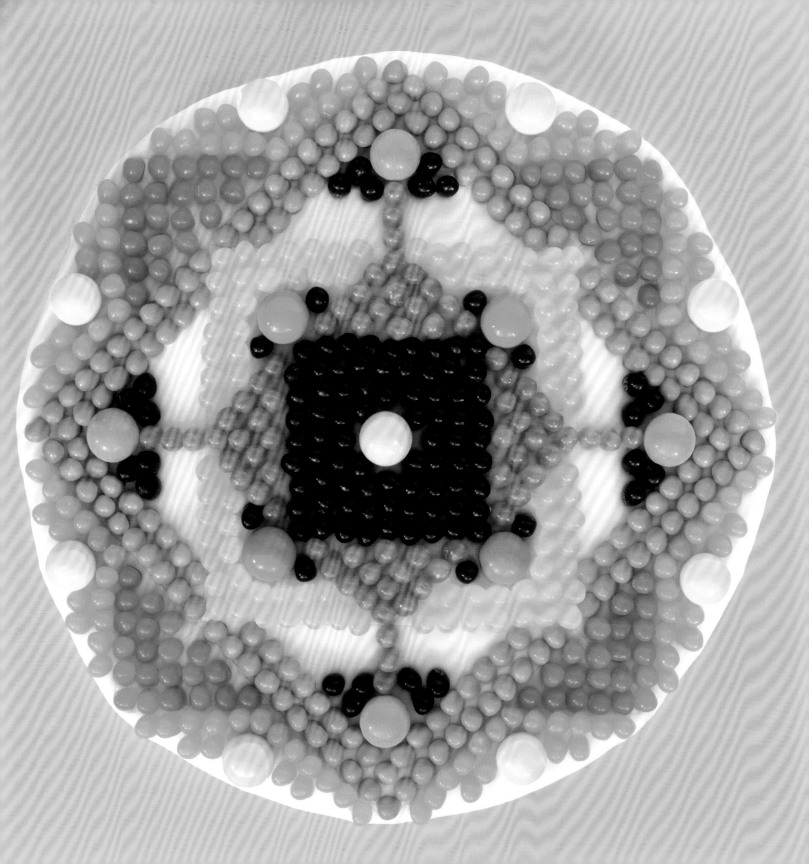

FIREWORK CAKE

23cm diameter

Ingredients

- Marzipan
- Yellow icing
- White icing
- Red icing
- White sugar balls
- Red sugar balls
- Red sugar pearls
- Red chocolate hearts
- Red writing icing
- Red glacé cherries
- Edible glue

All the main shapes are made of icing. There are red and white cut out shapes and rolled hemispheres of white icing stuck with red sugar balls. The whirligigs are made of sheets of red and white icing layered together, rolled up and sliced. Everything else is stuck on – until there is no room left!

Although it looks more like fireworks, this cake is loosely based on a scarf design of mine called 'Bouquet'. It was fun making something so three dimensional out of a flat pattern – it looks almost like hills and valleys in the close up.

ADULTS' BIRTHDAYS

KIMONO CAKE

23cm diameter

Ingredients
– Marzipan
– Yellow icing
– Black icing
– Black sugar balls in two sizes
– Edible glue

Getting the design perfectly symmetrical
is probably the most difficult task here.
Once you have pricked it out onto the icing
it is just a matter of following the lines.
The central flourishes are cut out of black
icing and the rest is just sugar balls. In any
one packet there is quite a variation in size
so I spent ages sorting them out in order
to have them graded from big to little.

*I recently went to an
exhibition of Sakai
Hoitsu, a Japanese
painter of the late 18th
and early 19th centuries.
Among the many
extraordinary works on
show I noticed a recurring
circular motif beautifully
portrayed on the kimonos,
which I took note of and
have reproduced here.*

VALENCIA TILE

26cm square

Ingredients
- Marzipan
- White icing
- Black icing
- Blue icing
- Gold edible paint
- Gold sugar balls
- Black sugar balls
- Edible glue

This cake needs a bit of skill to fit the icing shapes together neatly. The central square is black; the border consists of two adjacent sides of black and two of white, painted gold. The blue rolled icing borders help contain the black and gold sugar balls, which are faded into one another to create a three-dimensional effect.

There is a traditional Valencian tile design of a diagonally bisected square. It is used to make many patterns but the addition of a more elaborate version to the mix makes a much grander scheme. This cake is based on that special tile.

BLUEBIRDS

26cm square

Ingredients

– Marzipan
– Blue icing
– White icing
– Black writing icing
– Blue writing icing
– Yellow glacé cherries
– White sugar balls
– Blue sugar polka dots
– Gold sugar balls
– Edible glue

This cake has a background of yellow marzipan. The blue birds and white circle are cut out of icing using templates as a guide. Writing icing is used to emphasise the shape of the birds and to outline the circle but you could use rolled strips of icing instead.

Birds are a recurring theme in my work. They can be stylised so easily and make great shapes. With a bit of ingenuity they can even be made to fit into a corner so they work well on this square cake.

GOLDFISH

23cm diameter

Ingredients

- Marzipan
- Blue icing
- Orange icing
- Black icing
- Edible gold paint
- Blue non-pareils
- Green non-pareils
- Candied orange peel
- Gold sugar balls
- Blue sugar balls
- Black sugar balls
- Edible glue

The goldfish are cut out of orange icing and then decorated with candied orange peel once they have been stuck on the cake. The 'swooshes' are added by painting on edible glue and pouring the non-pareils over it. The surplus can be dusted away once the glue has dried. The gold paint and random gold balls are added as finishing touches.

As with birds I always find fishes make a pleasing decorative motif. I have used them successfully on fabrics and lampshades, so why not on a cake?

JERMYN STREET

30cm diameter

Ingredients
- Marzipan
- Grey icing
- Blue icing
- White icing
- Glacé kiwi slices
- Edible gold leaf
- Silver sugar balls
- Edible glue

The various shades of grey used here were mixed by hand, the black and blue icing being gradually added to ready-mixed white. It takes quite a lot of kneading to get an even colour. The two background colours are cut into 6cm strips and then butted up to make a flat stripey base for the raised strips. The kiwi squares are very sticky so the gold leaf adheres easily.

I wanted to do something masculine and chic here, so I decided to stick with shades of grey in elegant stripes. The design is reminiscent of my front hall which is decorated in grey stripes and gold spots.

INDIAN STRIPE

50 × 28cm approx.

Ingredients
- White icing
- Purple icing
- Red icing
- Angelica
- Glacé red pears
- Green glacé cherries
- Gold sugar balls
- Red sugar balls
- Turquoise sugar balls
- Edible glue

I created this cake for my brother's birthday party. It is made of two bought 'mega tray bakes' with added chocolate filling. The decoration is not difficult but it is rather painstaking. You need to measure your cake and work out how it divides up. After the initial icing you then mark out the plan and stick the coloured icing rectangles into place. Then it is a matter of filling the gaps with coloured balls, angelica and glacé fruit. The sides can be a little tricky – leave the glue to get tacky before sticking on the decorations – and keep in place with pins if necessary.

This design is a straight nick from one of my most popular scarf designs called 'Indian Stripe'. That, in turn was inspired by going to India, where all my favourite fabrics were stripey. Interestingly, when executed in icing and baubles it is reminiscent of tapestry and looks rather like a hassock.

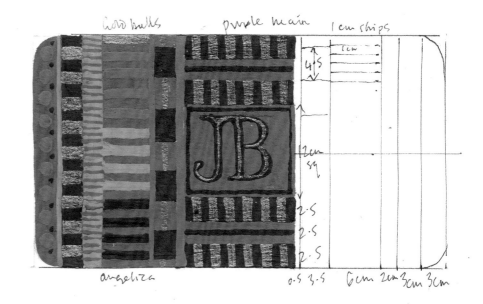

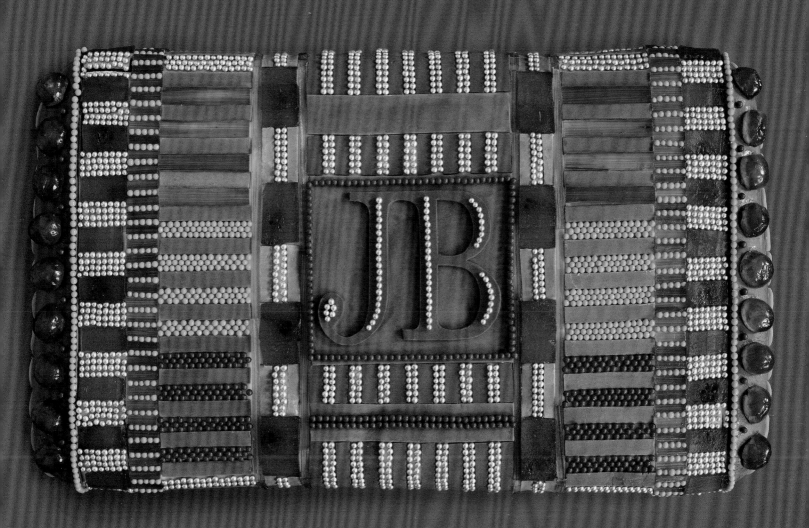

ROMANCE

HEART BOARD

25cm diameter

Ingredients

- Marzipan
- White icing
- Red icing
- Pink icing
- Blue icing
- Angelica
- Gold chocolate hearts
- Gold sugar balls
- Pink non-pareils
- Turquoise non-pareils
- Edible glue

The red circles need to be dried until firm in order to transfer them to the cake. Use a circle of card to shift them, adjusting any distortion while sticking them down. The pink circles and blue oblongs are covered with matching non-pareils. Glue the surface and place them face down in a saucer of the tiny beads. You could leave this stage out if it's just too fiddly. The rest is just a matter of sticking everything down in a radiating pattern continuing down the sides.

Concentric circles are an obvious solution for a round cake decoration. In red and white they have quite a graphic impact which is softened here with added hearts to make a delicious Valentine.

CRESCENT MOON

30cm diameter

Ingredients

- Marzipan
- White icing
- Turquoise icing
- Dark blue icing
- Silver sugar balls
- Edible silver starlets
- Edible glue

The white stars were all cut out first using templates and then allowed to dry. I fitted the three colours of icing together so that they are on the same level, but it would probably be easier starting with a dark blue ground and sticking the white crescent and turquoise border on top. After positioning the white stars sprinkle some of the tiny silver starlets around them like stardust.

A crescent moon makes a magical decoration for a cake. Here I have picked it out in silver against a dark blue ground with a myriad of surrounding stars.

BLOOMSBURY BOUQUET

30cm diameter

Ingredients

- Marzipan
- Angelica
- Glacé pineapple
- Glacé kiwi
- Candied orange peel
- Red glacé pears
- Yellow glacé pears
- Red glacé cherries
- Mauve jelly beans
- Black sugar balls
- Edible glue

This cake needs a bit of flair and imagination. It tastes great as there is no icing involved and all the flowers are made of fruit and sweets. You need to consider which would be good for what; the cores of the pears look like stamens and the orange peel makes great petals. The leaves are made of either angelica or glacé kiwis and the stems and vase from marzipan tinted with food colouring. The addition of the black sugar balls is a design trick to add a bit more depth and impact.

Children should have fun cutting out the flowers and leaves from glacé fruit and angelica.

This design is an adaptation of my 'Flower Vase' cushion which I originally designed for a client in the USA who is a collector of Bloomsbury Group paintings and artefacts.

HEART'S DELIGHT

23cm diameter

Ingredients

- Marzipan
- Red icing
- Pink icing
- Yellow icing
- Pink writing icing
- Gold sugar balls
- Orange sugar balls
- Pale pink sugar balls
- Gold chocolate hearts
- Red chocolate heart
- Yellow rotella fruit wheel
- Edible glue

Once you have drawn this design on paper and transferred it to the cake you can then cut it up to make templates for the heart and the star. If you number the rays of the star it will help you position them correctly. The pattern on the pink heart needs to be pricked out separately and then created using the rotella fruit wheel and gold balls.

Every year I design a new Valentine card and this is a version of the one for 2012 (which has two hearts locked together). It has a definite Mexican flavour with the background star reminiscent of the one behind the Madonna of Guadalupe.

WEDDINGS

CROWN CAKE

30cm diameter

Ingredients

- Marzipan
- Red icing
- Red writing icing
- Blue icing
- White icing
- Edible disco glitter
- Edible gold paint
- Green metallic sugar balls
- Black sugar balls
- Sugar pearls in two sizes
- Isomalt jewels
- Pearl bubble gum gobstoppers
- Gilded sugar
- Edible glue

Everyday red icing is never a strong enough shade for me so here I used a deep red writing icing and disco glitter on top of the basic red icing to get a richer colour on this cake. The crown is cut out and gilded before sticking it down – using gold paint first and then the golden sugar. Once the crown is in place all the other decorations are added; strips of blue icing enhanced with glitter, lots of pearls and finally the gorgeous isomalt jewels.

I looked at many pictures of crowns to find a shape suitable for this cake. I wanted something magnificent and grand with plenty of sparkle, so when I was in the USA I sought out some special ingredients including these huge pearl gobstoppers and the gilded sugar. I hope these will soon be available everywhere.

DOUBLE DECKER

Base 30cm diameter
Top 20cm diameter
22cm tall

Ingredients

- Marzipan
- White icing
- Black icing
- Orange sugar balls
- Orange M&Ms
- Black sugar balls
- Orange gobstoppers
- Edible glue

It is easiest to decorate the base and top separately and then stick them together. You will need to measure around each cake and divide the number into five to find the size of the sunbursts. It is best to make the shapes out of their constituent parts – semicircles and oblongs – and stick them onto the cakes separately. Adding all the orange and black baubles is then just a nice mindless job.

This sunrise motif appears in quite a lot of my designs. It is a bit unusual to present it in black and orange, but it is a very striking colourway which I think works well.

DAISY CAKE

About 25cm diameter

Ingredients

- Marzipan
- White icing
- White candy sticks
- Pink non-pareils
- Lime green sugar balls
- Orange sugar balls
- Edible glue

The laborious part of this decoration is to prepare the candy sticks. Cut each 3cm stick in half lengthwise and cut each end into a point. You need about five hundred! Each flower is made of a ball of white icing cut in half, dipped in pink non-pareils and stuck with the candy 'petals'. Once they are stuck on the cake the lime green balls are rolled in like pin-balls.

For some reason it occurred to me to decorate a cake in the style of a fifties swimming hat. I messed about with some candy sticks and pink non-pareils and came up with this very over-the-top and slightly bonkers design.

KREMLIN CROWN

23cm diameter

Ingredients

– Marzipan
– Red icing
– Turquoise icing
– Sugar pearls
– Blue metallic sugar pearls
– Edible gold paint
– Isomalt jewels

If you have a cake where the top has risen this would be the perfect decoration. Otherwise you would need to build up the top into a mound with a delicious ingredient like marzipan or chocolate. The design needs to be transferred onto the icing using a pin and then marked out using sugar pearls. The isomalt gems have edible gold leaf stuck onto their backs while they are setting to give them extra shine.

As the name of this cake suggests this design was directly inspired by the wonderful crowns of the Tsars in the Kremlin Museum in Moscow. My niece, who was working there at the time I visited pointed out how much they reminded her of my cakes. So there was no escaping it…

SNOWFLAKE

30cm diameter

Ingredients
- Marzipan
- White icing
- Silver balls in three sizes
- Isomalt gems
- Edible glue

To start you need to fold a circle of paper into six. You then draw a sixth part of your snowflake design onto it and cut it out – like the doilies we all made when we were children. This pattern is used as a template for the second layer of white icing. The pattern is then enhanced using different sizes of silver balls in serried ranks with isomalt crystals as the final flourish.

We all love the intricacy of a real snowflake – and the fact that each one is unique. This pristine all-white design makes a beautiful icy looking wedding or Christmas cake.

CONGRATULATIONS

GOLD STAR

30cm diameter

Ingredients

- Marzipan
- White icing
- Black writing icing
- Red writing icing
- Gold chocolate dragees
- Gold chocolate hearts
- Gold sugar balls
- Red glacé cherries
- Red chocolate hearts
- Red sugar balls
- Red rotella fruit wheels
- Edible glue

You will need to map out the areas of this cake in black writing icing. Fill in the central star with lots of gold decorations and the radial sections with any red decorations you can find.

Children can be given a section or two each to decorate.

There's a bit of the 'Stars & Stripes' about this one I think, and it makes a good co-operative project. Once you have the central star in place you can divide the cake into sections and everyone gets to decorate one or two each.

SUMMER FRUIT STAR

35cm diameter

Ingredients

- Frosting or whipped cream
- Strawberries
- Blueberries
- Blackcurrants
- Raspberries
- Redcurrants

Cover the cake with frosting or whipped cream and arrange the fruit into a star shape. The strawberries are cut in half but everything else is left whole. Pile the centre with blackcurrants and raspberries and top with redcurrants on their stalks. Add a final sprinkling of icing sugar if you like. Eat soon before it collapses!

I love to decorate cakes with whatever fruit is in season. It is a quick and easy way to make a spectacular celebratory dessert which is fresh and healthy.

CHAMPION CAKE

23cm diameter

Ingredients
- Marzipan
- White icing
- Purple icing
- Yellow icing
- Red icing
- Mauve sugar pearls
- Yellow chocolate buttons
- Black sugar balls
- White candy sticks
- Yellow glacé cherry
- Mauve sugar ball
- Edible glue

The purple and yellow 'ribbons' are made of blocks of coloured icing laminated together and then sliced. Stick them on diagonally in a circle once they are dry enough to handle. The beads and baubles cover up the joins, as does the yellow ribbon at the bottom. Cut out the number or letters of your choice using a computer generated template and stick them on last.

This design occurred to me when casting about for circular imagery. Why not a prize rosette? Pretty and celebratory, they can be awarded for more or less anything and come in every colour. What is more you can add whatever writing you please – and all sorts of additional bling.

CHOCOLATE BOX

30 × 20cm approx.

Ingredients
- Chocolate fondant icing
- Chocolate orange segments
- Dark chocolate bars
- Milk chocolate bars
- White chocolate bars
- Matchmakers
- White chocolate buttons in two sizes
- White chocolate stars
- Edible gold leaf
- Edible glue

This a good way to decorate a bought tray-bake cake, adding plenty of chocolate value. You need to get an idea of what will fit where before icing the cake so you can cut up the chocolate bars to the right sizes. It is best to cut them from the back with a scalpel, ignoring the manufacturers divisions. The gold leaf is cut with scissors and stuck on last.

Children should be able to stick all the elements in place once the plan is drawn out.

I am not a big fan of the colour brown so chocolate presents particular problems as an ingredient for me. However, the chocolate cake cannot be left out so here I turned to Africa for inspiration. I love the geometric designs of the 'bark cloth' and thought I could put that influence to good use here.

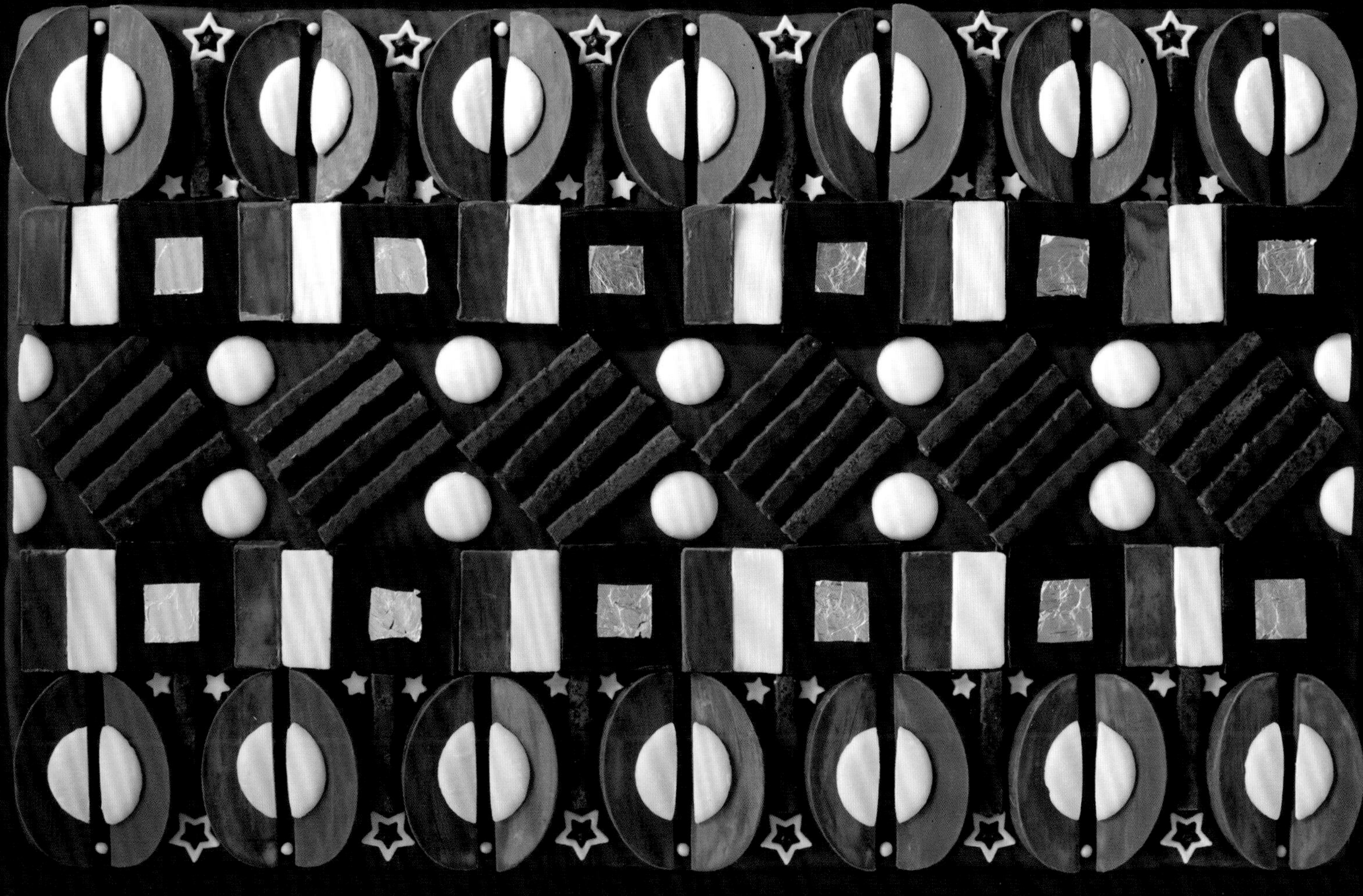

SPRING

SPRING LEAVES

30cm diameter

Ingredients
- Marzipan
- Pale blue icing
- Pale green icing
- Mid-green icing
- Black icing
- Tiny silver sugar balls
- Green sugar balls
- Pale green sugar polka dots
- Red sugar balls
- Edible glue

Divide the cake into sixteen and mark it accordingly so you can position the leaves. The central circle and leaves are cut out of shades of green icing using a template. Once they are stuck down use tapered black icing rolls on top of the leaves to form the stems. Finish with red sugar balls, silver balls and green sugar polka dots.

I painted a round table rather like this for my last book – and it does just as well on a cake in my opinion.

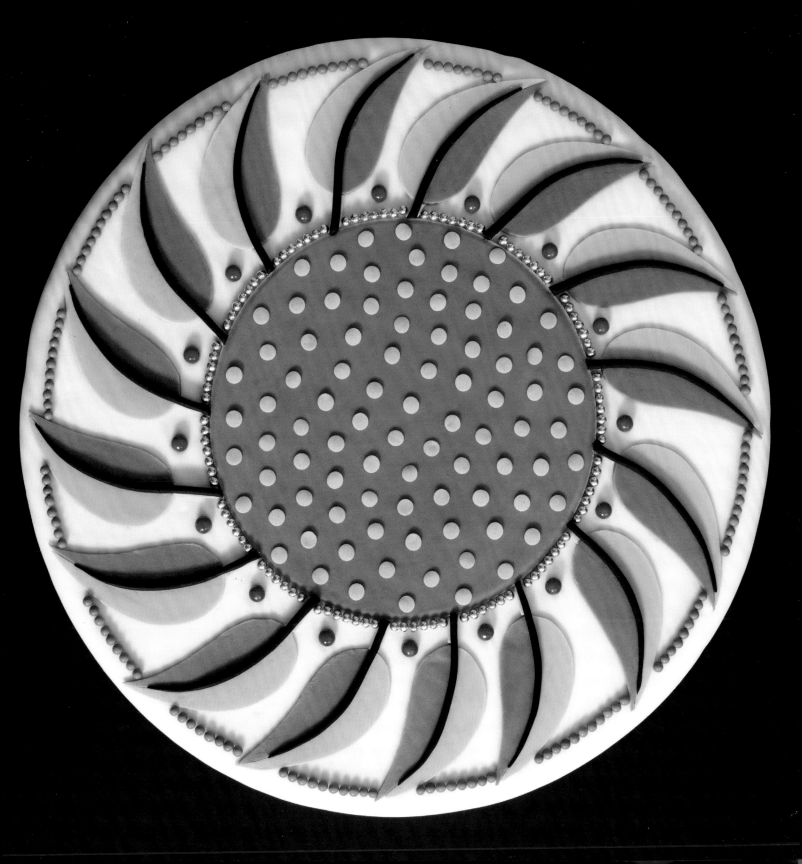

SPRINGTIME

30cm diameter

Ingredients

- Marzipan
- White icing
- Mauve icing
- Yellow icing
- White mimosa balls
- Blue sugar beads
- Pink sugar polka dots
- Edible glue

The egg shapes are made using a mould. In this case it was wooden but an Easter egg or a real one would be fine. The icing is wrapped around half of it and left until dry. It can then be cut off and decorated with cut-out icing shapes as shown here. The smaller eggs and hemispheres are made of solid icing shaped by hand.

I wanted to create a lovely springtime Easter cake here so I chose to make it in pastel shades with three-dimensional egg shapes. These ones are empty but you could hide a surprise chocolate or two inside each one!

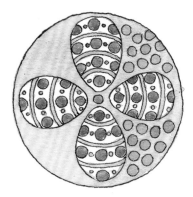

DAHLIA CAKE

23cm diameter

Ingredients

- – Pale green icing
- – Yellow icing
- – Angelica
- – Candied orange peel
- – Candied lemon peel
- – Yellow glacé cherries
- – White mimosa balls
- – White candy sticks
- – Orange sugar balls
- – Green sugar balls
- – Edible glue

Start from the outside with the yellow icing petals and angelica and work inwards, piling on the cut lengths of candied peel as you go. Make little stamens by cutting the candy sticks into slim lengths and poking them in around the centre of the flower.

Once you have done the outer petals children should be able to help with the rest.

The candied orange and lemon peel I buy is so delicious I wanted to think of a way to use it in quantity. This generic dahlia seems to do the trick by piling on layers of angelica, peel and cherries to make a delicious edible flower.

FRUIT FEAST

30 × 20cm approx.

Ingredients

- Frosting or whipped cream
- Kiwi fruit
- Strawberries
- Oranges
- Pineapple
- Grapes
- Nectarines

It is important to start by preparing your fruit properly. Peel them immaculately leaving no pith and then slice them finely. You can work out your design on a chopping board first if you like and then transfer the whole thing to the cake. It works very well as a dessert without a cake too!

These fruit are normally available all year round so this makes a good standby birthday cake or dessert. The cake consists of two ready-made tray-bake sponge cakes piled on top of one another, but of course you can make your own.

SUMMER

ORANGE LATTICE

30cm diameter

Ingredients

- Marzipan
- White icing
- Orange icing
- Turquoise icing
- Pale green icing
- Pale orange icing
- Black writing icing
- Orange M&Ms
- White sugar balls
- Turquoise sugar balls
- Orange sugar balls
- Edible glue

The orange and turquoise icing are cut from templates and should fit together. Once they have firmed up they can be transferred to the cake quite easily using a circle of card as a support. The lattice is made from strips cut out of black icing. Positioning them is the most difficult part; do the first layer in one direction, then lay the second on top. Cut the strips off at an angle to fit.

When I was little there was a plate at my grandparents' house, Charleston, which we children all fought over. I don't remember it clearly except that it was turquoise, orange and black with cross-hatching and flowers. This is an attempt to replicate that plate.

PEACOCK CAKE

30cm diameter

Ingredients

- Marzipan
- White icing
- Gold sugar balls
- Silver sugar balls
- Blue metallic sugar balls
- Green metallic sugar balls
- Glacé kiwis
- Green glacé cherries
- Gold chocolate hearts
- Turquoise writing icing
- Edible gold leaf
- Edible glue

Once you have drawn this design and transferred it onto the cake you will need to outline it using writing icing. Then all you need to do is fill in with the green cherries (cut into slices), gold balls and gilded kiwis. Finish with an edging of metallic sugar balls.

Get the children to fill the tail with gold balls and hearts.

A couple of years ago I saw two wonderful red woollen shawls in a museum in Edinburgh which featured rather disarming looking peacocks with very fancy tails. This one is rather less elaborate and a different colour but I hope it still has a bit of their charm.

CARNATION

30cm diameter

Ingredients

- Marzipan
- White icing
- Red icing
- Blue icing
- Black sugar balls
- Red sugar balls
- White sugar pearls
- Red glacé cherries
- Edible glue

When you are ready to stick on the icing shapes bear in mind that you need to leave a gap between the pieces so as to leave space for the black sugar balls. Stick on the white pearls, gradually thinning them out as you go.

This is a classic Ottoman design to be found all over Turkish pottery, tiles and textiles. I love it as a motif and originally used it in a textile pattern before it became a cake.

CHERRY TREE

30cm diameter

Ingredients
- Marzipan
- White icing
- Red icing
- Green icing
- Black icing
- Yellow icing
- Red glacé cherries
- Dark red glacé cherries
- Tiny silver sugar balls
- Edible glue

Once you have the design on paper you can then prick it out onto the white icing. Then you have to start rolling out the black icing to make the branches, tapering the ends and sticking them into place. The leaves are rather cunningly created by cutting each side with a metal bottle top. After they have dried you can place them naturalistically along the boughs and around the circumference of the cake.

This tree is adapted from a wall hanging design I did for a Lutyens house. It is so emphatically circular that it always looked as though it would be an excellent cake decoration. Although I love the result it was a long task to re-create the tree in icing and I might think twice about doing it again!

AUTUMN

MELLOW FRUIT

25cm diameter

Ingredients

- Glacé pineapple
- Glacé red pears
- Glacé yellow pears
- Crystallised apricots
- Candied lemon peel
- Glacé kiwis
- Crystallised figs
- Crystallised mandarins
- Red glacé cherries
- Green glacé cherries
- Dark red glacé cherries
- Glacé melon
- Pecan nuts
- Edible gold leaf
- Dried currants
- Angelica
- Edible glue
- Ready-made jelly

There is no icing or marzipan on this cake, just an apricot glaze and some edible glue to stick down the pieces of fruit that don't stick themselves. Use the big fruit to create a structure for your design and then fill in the gaps with cherries, currants, strips of angelica and gilded pecans. A layer of melted pre-made jelly fills in the holes and adds a gloss.

Once you have the main design in place the children can fill in with cherries and the other smaller fruit.

I enjoy creating delicious icing-free toppings for fruit cakes. What you use all depends on what ingredients you can get hold of. Once you have amassed your glacé fruits and gilded nuts, just think Carmen Miranda – and make a gorgeous fruity design.

FRUTERO

26cm square

Ingredients

- Marzipan
- White icing
- Yellow icing
- Blue icing
- Green icing
- Yellow glacé cherries
- Dark red glacé cherries
- Red glacé cherries
- Crystallised mandarins
- Crystallised figs
- Green acid drops
- Angelica
- Glacé pineapple
- Liquorice wheels
- Edible glue

This is the solution for a cake that has sunk in the middle. If it hasn't then you will need to make a thick layer of marzipan and carve out a bowl in the centre before putting it onto the cake. The leaves are made by cutting around actual leaves and the stalks are pieces of angelica or liquorice split and stuck into the glacé fruit.

Children should enjoy arranging the glacé cherries to form bunches of grapes.

I had in mind a beautiful Italian platter of my sister's which is in yellow and blue with a bunch of grapes painted in the middle. Here I reproduce it but with actual glacé fruit in the bowl.

THANKSGIVING CAKE

30cm diameter

Ingredients

- Marzipan
- Orange icing
- Green icing
- Red icing
- Maroon icing
- Angelica
- Candied orange peel
- Candied lemon peel
- Crystallised apricots
- Crystallised figs
- Natural red glacé cherries
- Yellow glacé cherries
- Green glacé cherries
- Hazelnuts
- Raisins
- Dried cranberries
- Bronze sugar balls
- Edible glue
- Edible glaze

Underneath the leaves there is a circle of marzipan (or icing) which stops the whole thing looking flat. The leaf shapes are printed out from ready-made shapes on my computer – but they could be copied from real leaves. Cut out more than enough of each colour so that you can pick and choose as you build up the design. The finished cake is given a gloss with a spray of edible glaze.

This is an icing version of a Thanksgiving wreath with multi-coloured Autumn leaves, fruit and nuts.

FRUIT AND NUT

25cm diameter

Ingredients

- Glacé pineapple
- Glacé kiwi
- Edible gold leaf
- Pecans
- Blanched almonds
- Crystallised mandarins
- Red glacé cherries
- Green glacé cherries
- Angelica
- Gold sugar balls
- Edible glue
- Blackcurrant conserve

I started with the pineapple ring in the middle, gilding it on the back to make it shine. Working outwards, add rings of fruit (which should stick themselves) and gilded nuts. To finish fill in any gaps with blackcurrant conserve, which looks rich and tastes delicious.

This is pretty easy for children to help with except for gilding the nuts.

This is one of the easiest cakes in the book; no icing or marzipan, just glacé fruit and nuts in concentric circles. Choose any fruit you like the look of and add a splash of gold to make it more festive.

CHRISTMAS

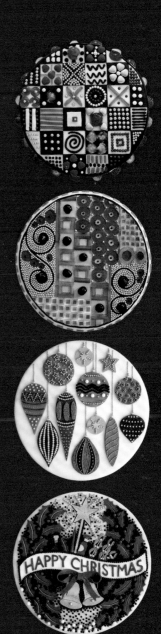

CHEQUERBOARD

23cm diameter

Ingredients

- Marzipan
- White icing
- Black icing
- Black writing icing
- Angelica
- Green glacé cherries
- Red glacé cherries
- Yellow glacé cherries
- Gold sugar balls
- Silver sugar balls
- Red sugar balls
- White sugar balls in two sizes
- Gold chocolate hearts
- Red chocolate hearts
- Edible glue

Once you have created the chequerboard top you just need to employ imagination to think of different patterns for each square. Continuing the check pattern down the sides won't work on a circle but you can make a border of white and black squares and decorate them with cherries.

Everyone can join in with this one. Allocate a number of squares to each to decorate.

I have done versions of this before, but that was when my nephews and nieces were eager to join in with decorating the cake. Once you have divided the cake into checks (or some other geometric shape) each square can be decorated separately. Personally I prefer to limit the colours of decorations available to prevent things looking too messy.

KLIMT CAKE

30cm diameter

Ingredients

- Marzipan
- Gold sugar balls
- Black sugar balls
- Angelica
- Red glacé pears
- Glacé melon
- Glacé kiwis
- Dark red glacé cherries
- Liquorice wheels
- Edible gold paint
- Edible glue

NB. The gold sugar balls used here turned silver overnight for no known reason!

Once you have marked out the design, apply a couple of coats of edible gold paint to the central part of the cake where the angelica and glacé pears will go. Cut all the glacé fruit to fit; the most fiddly bit is the check area of glacé melon, pear and angelica. If you keep your knife wetted with hot water it will make it easier and less sticky. Use liquorice for the black lines.

I designed this cake after a visit to Prague. Although Klimt was not actually Czech they seem to have adopted him and we saw imagery from his work everywhere. I love the geometric textiles in his paintings and this is my take on them.

BAUBLES CAKE

30cm diameter

Ingredients

- Marzipan
- White icing
- Blue icing
- Pink icing
- Red icing
- Orange icing
- Green icing
- Turquoise icing
- Red and blue disco glitter
- Big, medium and tiny silver balls
- Gold sugar balls
- White sugar pearls
- White chocolate stars painted gold
- Metallic green sugar balls
- Metallic blue sugar balls
- Black sugar balls
- Red sugar balls
- Pink non-pareils
- Edible gold and silver starlets
- Edible glue

Make templates for the different bauble shapes and cut them out in different colours of icing. Decorate each according to your whim with plenty of glitter and shimmer. This is a good way to use up spare bits and pieces as each bauble can be different. Pick out the chains with tiny silver balls and use the biggest ones you can find for the metal fittings.

Before they are stuck down each different bauble can be handed to a child to decorate as they please.

This design has a definite fifties flavour, probably influenced by an old Christmas card I was once sent. My memory of all the glass baubles we had on the tree when I was young is quite distinct and these decorations hark back to some of them.

NOEL CAKE

30cm diameter

Ingredients

- Marzipan
- White icing
- Red icing
- Dark green icing
- Pale green icing
- Gold sugar balls
- Black sugar balls
- White mimosa
- Red sugar balls
- White sugar pearls
- Edible gold paint
- Edible black paint or food colouring
- Edible glue

This is rather time-consuming to make. The holly leaves and berries are an easy beginning but once you get involved in mistletoe, stars and bells things start to get complicated. The bow is fairly simply constructed from loops of icing and the gold stars and bells are made from icing painted gold. The black balls are packed in at the end to give contrast and depth.

Here I am trying to please the traditionalist with holly, bells, bows and stars in profusion. The overall design is based on a Christmas card I designed some time ago which was meant to have a hint of Victoriana.

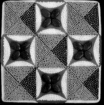

CELEBRATIONS

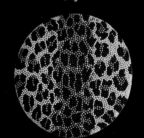

CIRCLE CAKE

23cm diameter

Ingredients

- Marzipan
- Pink icing
- Black writing icing
- Black sugar balls
- Green sugar balls
- Green M&Ms
- Turquoise M&Ms
- Silver sugar balls
- Turquoise non-pareils
- Green non-pareils
- Glacé cherries in two shades of red
- Edible glue

Once you have arranged your circles on the cake and marked them out it is plain sailing to fill them with the various decorations using tweezers and glue.

Children can each be given their own circles to fill in.

This simple idea of an arrangement of circles allows for plenty of scope to add decorations in any style or colour you like.

BLUE NOTE

26cm square

Ingredients

- Marzipan
- White icing
- Three shades of blue icing
- Three shades of blue sugar balls
- Dark blue chocolate dragees
- White sugar balls
- Edible glue

After working out the design on paper and transferring it to the cake you can cut out the constituent parts to make paper templates. Each square is made of one dark blue, one light blue and two mid-blue triangles. To stick on the sugar balls make a triangular cardboard 'cookie-cutter' to contain the balls as you pour them in.

I found a small image of blue and white tiles in this configuration when researching della Robbia online. I was very taken with the design, so soon found myself adapting it for a cake decoration.

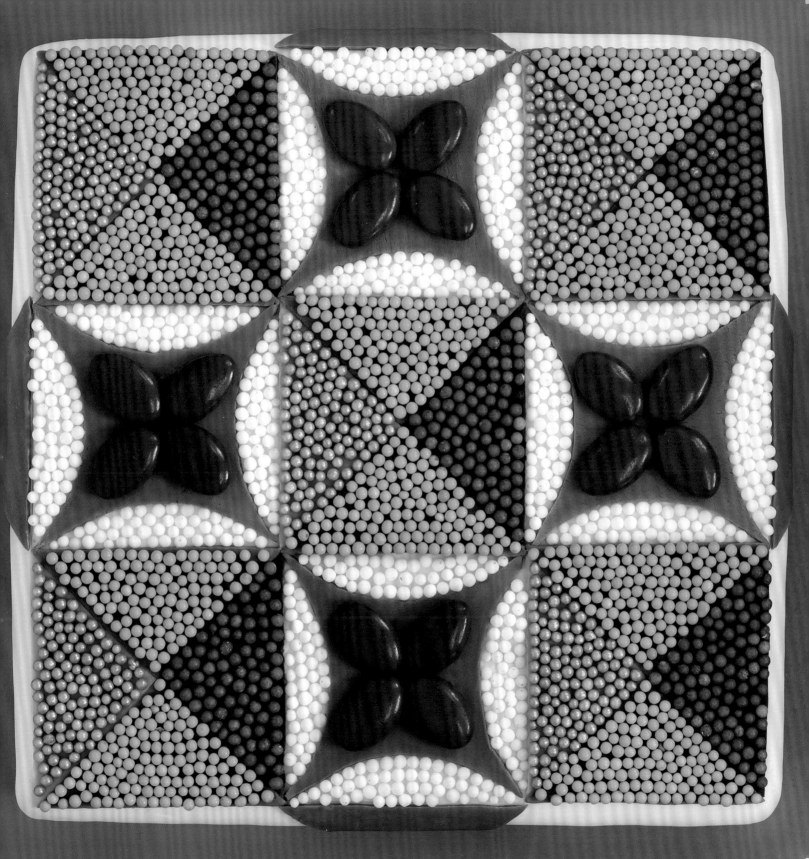

CHOCOLATE FLOWERS

25cm diameter

Ingredients

- Chocolate frosting
- Thornton's praline flower melts
- Thornton's caramel melts
- Chocolate raisins
- Giant dark chocolate buttons
- White chocolate buttons in two sizes
- Milk chocolate buttons
- Nestlé's Vice Versas
- Galaxy Counters
- Chocolate Crispies
- White mimosa balls

I cut most of the buttons in half – which can be hard to do, especially with the Vice Versas which have a hard candy coating. They do look good though; their thin white edges contrast nicely with the other solid coloured chocolates. It is a bit wasteful to only use two of the stripey caramels but I feel sure the others will always find a home!

I am full of admiration for the chocolatier's art and would not even attempt anything along those lines. Instead I bought lots of different chocolate buttons and invented a design around them. Using them end-up seemed the less obvious route to take and made a great pattern.

INDIAN PAISLEY

25cm diameter

Ingredients

- Marzipan
- Turquoise icing
- Purple icing
- Gold sugar balls
- Tiny silver sugar balls
- Turquoise sugar balls
- Blue dragees
- Purple sugar pearls
- Gold chocolate hearts
- Gold chocolate buttons
- Blue isomalt jewels
- Red jelly jewels
- Edible glue

The turquoise icing shapes are stuck on to the purple background, outlined in tiny silver balls and decorated with gold balls. The sides are embellished with alternating blue dragees and purple sugar pearls. The isomalt jewels are backed with gold leaf to add glitter and are stuck on last.

The ancient paisley or 'boteh' pattern is a textile designers' staple so has to be included here. This arrangement of paisleys is based on one of my scarves called 'Ottoman', but the colour scheme looks more Indian with all its gold and jewels.

LEOPARD CAKE

25cm diameter

Ingredients

- Marzipan
- Gold sugar balls
- Bronze sugar balls
- Black sugar balls
- Edible glue

This is a labour of love! The design comes from a photo which I simplified to three colours. Once it is pricked out onto the marzipan base, use tweezers to place the three colours of sugar balls in place, glueing as you go. I faded out the spots as they went down the sides because I ran out of steam. Allow a couple of days for this one.

I can hardly claim any originality for this design – it is a perennial favourite among designers of all persuasions. The treatment here is a little different though and is inspired by an amazing leopard skin dress I bought made entirely of sequins.

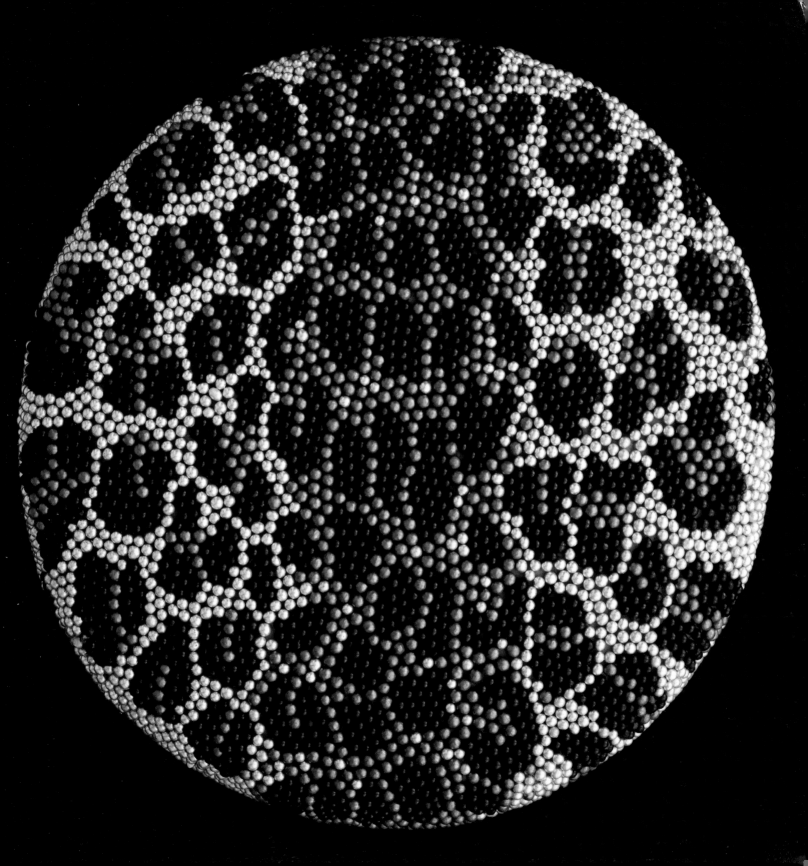

FLEUR DE LYS

30cm diameter

Ingredients
- Marzipan
- White icing
- Blue icing
- Food colouring
- Cloves
- Black icing
- Edible glue

The plain white marzipan is coloured to make varying shades of green. The different shapes of leaves are then cut out and arranged around the edge to form a wreath. The blackberries are made up of tiny balls of black icing; all the other fruit is marzipan painted with food colouring. Cloves are stuck in to look like stalks.

I have always loved the ceramic roundels made by Luca della Robbia in the 15th Century. They look to me as if they were made to be cakes with their lovely fruit and leaf borders. I decided against a sheep or a Madonna and Child in the centre and settled instead for a simpler fleur de lys design in his signature blue and white.

LIST OF SUPPLIERS

This list includes the suppliers I used for this book to give you an indication of where to find what. It is by no means comprehensive and you may well prefer others that you find either locally or on the internet. Items in stock change rapidly so shop around if you can't immediately find what you want.

GENERAL DECORATING SUPPLIES

All sorts of equipment and materials including coloured icings, marzipan, sugar sprinkles, dragees, sugar balls, sugar pearls, chocolate hearts, sugar polka dots, mimosa, glitter, edible glue, edible paints, edible gold leaf, isomalt, sugar gems, printed icing, non-pareils etc.

www.cakecraftshop.co.uk
www.thecakedecoratingcompany.co.uk
www.edible-glitter.co.uk
www.lakeland.co.uk
www.squires-shop.com

A M Sugarcraft Ltd
136 Upper Richmond Rd, London, SW14 8DS
Tel. 020 8392 1647

The Dalston Party Party Shop
9-13 Ridley Road, London, E8 2NP
Tel. 0207 254 5168

The Kilburn Party Party Shop
206 Kilburn High Road, London, NW6 4JH
Tel. 0207 624 4295

Sugarshack
Unit 12, Bowman's Trading Estate,
Westmoreland Road, London NW9 9RL
Tel. 020 8204 2994

Jane Asher Party Cakes & Sugarcraft
22-24 Cale Street, London, SW3 3QU
Tel. 020 7584 6177

Home Cake Decorating Supply Company
9514 Roosevelt Way NE, Seattle, WA 98115. USA
Tel. 001 206 522-4300

Also bigger branches of supermarket chains

SWEETS AND CHOCOLATES

Liquorice Allsorts, liquorice wheels, coconut rolls, bubble gum millions, candy sticks, fondant creams, refreshers, flying saucers, gobstoppers, chocolate buttons, midget gems, glacier fruits, rotella wheels, chocolate buttons etc.

www.thepinksugarmouse.com
www.chocolatebuttons.co.uk
www.realfoods.co.uk
www.aquarterof.co.uk
www.loveofliquorice.co.uk

Mrs Kibble's Olde Sweet Shoppe
57a Brewer St. London W1F 9UL
Tel. 0333 123 2345

Suck and Chew
130 Columbia Rd, London E2 7RG
Tel. 020 8983 3504

Also bigger branches of supermarket chains

JELLY BEANS

See www.jellybelly-uk.com for shops stocking the full range

CRYSTALLISED AND GLACÉ FRUIT

Cherries, clementines, pears, figs, pineapples, kiwi slices, melons, peaches, pineapples, apricots, candied peel, angelica etc.

www.buywholefoodsonline.co.uk
www.countryproducts.co.uk

Fortnum & Mason
181 Piccadilly, London W1A 1ER
Tel. 0845 300 1707

SUGARED AND CANDIED FLOWERS

Violas, pansies, snapdragons, mini roses, lavender, cornflowers, primroses, violas, geraniums etc.

www.crystallizedflowers.com
www.meadowsweetflowers.co.uk

INDEX

ACKNOWLEDGMENTS

I would very much like to thank Caroline Clifton-Mogg who came up with the idea for this project. Since first glimpsing one of my cakes she knew there was a book waiting to be produced. In the end she set up Double-Barrelled Books (with Meredith Etherington-Smith) and did it herself! She has been a driving force throughout and with Meredith has been a great source of encouragement and enthusiasm.

My assistant Minnie-Mae Stott has been invaluable. Her skill with a rolling pin and a pair of tweezers is impressive and her participation in the process has made our cake-decorating days over the last year a real pleasure. She is also a great cook and she baked many of the cakes shown here.

I am indebted to Sonja Read who spent many long hours at my studio photographing the cakes for this book. The care and attention she took is evident and I am delighted with the result. I also owe thanks to renowned food stylist Peta O'Brien who stepped into the breach to help with the surprisingly difficult task of cake slicing.

Finally I want to thank my partner for putting up with my endless cake-obsessive conversation while doing this book and, latterly, for his patience in reading and correcting my text. He was also a considerable help in the task of cake-eating for which I am extremely grateful!

Cressida Bell